# The Little Black Book of Stock Market Secrets

## Powerful Strategies for Building Wealth

Matthew R. Kratter

**http://www.trader.university**

For Kyriana

# Disclaimer

Neither Little Cash Machines LLC, nor any of its directors, officers, shareholders, personnel, representatives, agents, or independent contractors (collectively, the "Operator Parties") are licensed financial advisers, registered investment advisers, or registered broker-dealers. None of the Operator Parties are providing investment, financial, legal, or tax advice, and nothing in this book or at www.trader.university (henceforth, "the Site") should be construed as such by you. This book and the Site should be used as educational tools only and are not replacements for professional investment advice. The full disclaimer can be found at the end of this book.

# Table of Contents

# Your Free Gift

Thanks for purchasing my book!

As a way of showing my appreciation, I've created a **FREE BONUS CHAPTER** that includes even more trading strategies and market wisdom.

In this Bonus Chapter, you will learn:

- The single most important factor that drives the markets in the short term
- How to profit from the stock market's seasonality
- What happens to the stock market when all experts agree
- How to pick the best stock in a given industry
- And much, much more

Enter your email at the link below, and I will send you a free copy of this Bonus Chapter:

http://www.trader.university/secrets

# Chapter 1: Anyone Can Learn How to Trade

The book that you are holding in your hands is a veritable gold mine of trading secrets and strategies.

It's exactly the book that I wish I'd had when I was first learning how to trade.

I've been trading for over 20 years now, and during that time, I've had the opportunity to make every mistake in the book, as well as the blessing to have had many big winners.

When you hear someone say "The stock market is rigged" or "Trading stocks is too risky," you can be sure that you are in the presence of someone who has not put in the time and effort necessary to learn how the stock market really works.

You, on the other hand, are clearly different. You are destined for something greater.

You purchased this book because something in the title, cover, or book description resonated with you.

You know that trading is a skill that can be learned. And you are ready to put in the hard work to make it happen.

The market is not your friend, but it is also not your enemy. It is more like the waves on the ocean, or the heat from a fire-- just waiting to be harnessed by the savvy mind.

The stock market is the biggest opportunity machine ever created.

Read this book slowly, and let its lessons sink in.

Read it again after you've had your first big losing trade.

And read it whenever you're just looking for a little inspiration.

Also feel free to drop me a line at matt@trader.university. I'm here to help you on your journey to become a professional trader, and I respond to every email personally.

# Chapter 2: The Two Kinds of Markets, and How to Trade Them

There are only 2 kinds of markets: **trending** and **sideways**.

Knowing which kind of market you are in can be the difference between trading success and failure.

A **trending market** is one that keeps moving in the same direction (whether up or down) for an extended period of time.

## Uptrends

Strong uptrends often start with a burst of momentum, like a rocket blasting off. This initial burst of momentum can be a gap-up in prices (usually on higher than average volume), or even a long bullish candlestick.

In an uptrend, you should try to buy high and sell higher. Buy when a stock closes above the top Bollinger Band (try using a period=80), and then exit when it closes below the middle Bollinger Band.

In a strong uptrend, oscillators (like RSI or Stochastics) will stay "overbought" for an extended period of time. If you try to short a stock because it is overbought, you will lose money.

If a company continues to report strong revenues or earnings growth and the overall market is in an uptrend, you should be very wary about shorting a stock, especially if it continues to hit new 52-week highs.  Many a brokerage account has been blown up by doing this. Definitely don't try to short a stock if it gaps up to new highs after reporting good news.

Every stock that goes up a lot hits many new 52-week highs and all-time highs along the way.  If the trend is strong, do not be afraid to buy a stock at an all-time new high, especially if it is trading higher on greater than daily average volume.

Always trade in the direction of the trend.  In a strong daily uptrend, buy pullbacks on a 30-minute chart, or buy strong breakouts in the direction of the trend.

In a strong uptrend, a stock will trade above its 50-day moving average most of the time, and its 50-day moving average will trade above its 200-day moving average.

The first warning sign occurs when a stock drops below its 50-day moving average.  The second warning sign occurs when the stock drops below its 200-day moving average, or its 50-day moving average crosses below its 200-day moving average ("the Death Cross").  Most stock crashes happen after these 2 warning signs, so you will usually have no excuse if you are still in a stock that crashes.

### Downtrends

Strong downtrends often start with a burst of downward momentum, like a rocket crashing into the earth.  This initial burst of momentum can be a gap-down in prices (usually on higher than average volume), or even a long bearish candlestick.

In a downtrend, you should try to sell low ("sell short") and buy back ("buy to cover") lower. Go short when a stock closes below the lower Bollinger Band (period=80), and then cover your short when it closes back above the middle Bollinger Band.

In a strong downtrend, oscillators (like RSI or Stochastics) will stay "oversold" for an extended period of time. If you try to buy a down-trending stock because it is "oversold," you will lose money.

If a company has been reporting bad news and the overall market is in a downtrend, you should be very wary about buying its stock, especially if it continues to hit new 52-week lows. Be especially wary if the stock gaps down after reporting bad earnings or bad news.

Always trade in the direction of the trend. In a strong daily downtrend, short rallies on a 30-minute chart, or sell strong breakdowns in the direction of the trend.

In a strong downtrend, a stock will trade below its 50-day moving average most of the time, and its 50-day moving average will trade below its 200-day moving average.

The first sign that a stock is bottoming occurs when the stock trades above its 50-day moving average. The second sign occurs when the stock trades above its 200-day moving average, or its 50-day moving average crosses above its 200-day moving average ("the Golden Cross").

Most large rallies happen after these 2 signals, which will give you plenty of time to buy the stock at the start of its new uptrend.

***

The trend is your friend. Always trade in the direction of the trend, whether you are trading a 30-minute chart, a daily chart, or a weekly chart.

The trend is not your friend when it is about to end. If a trend has being going on for a long time and is being widely covered in the media, stay away.

An aging trend can end abruptly, causing widespread damage. If everyone is certain that a trend will continue, that means that the last possible buyer (seller) has already bought (sold). The only possible direction is then down (up).

If you notice a trend and tell other people about it, and you get strange looks or disapproval, the trend is near its beginning and you have a gold mine on your hands.

If other people enthusiastically agree with you, the trend is probably almost over.

If doctors, dentists, lawyers, or shoeshine boys are enthusiastically talking about a stock, the trend is over. Stay away from it.

Don't make big trades that depend on the ending of a trend. The market can remain irrational longer than you can remain solvent. It's better to sit in cash on the sidelines.

To learn more about trading with the trend, please see my books Rocket Stocks and Learn to Trade Momentum Stocks at www.trader-books.com

\*\*\*

The other kind of market is a **sideways** (also known as a "range-bound") market.

In a sideways market, prices do not trend up or down. They will often trade in a range, and your job is to try to buy at the lower end of this range, and sell at the upper end of this range.

A sideways market may trade between an upper price level ("resistance") and a lower price level ("support"). Or it may trade between its lower Bollinger Band and its upper Bollinger Band.

In an uptrend, you want to buy high and sell higher. But in a sideways market, you want to buy low and sell high. Buy when the stock closes below the lower Bollinger Band (period=80), and then sell when it closes above the middle (or even upper) Bollinger Band.

This is especially effective when trader sentiment is quite negative at the time that the stock closes below the lower Bollinger Band. For more on this strategy, see my book Rubber Band Stocks at www.trader-books.com.

In a sideways market, you want to buy when the RSI or Stochastics is oversold, and you want to sell when these oscillators become overbought again. It can be very satisfying to milk a stock for profits like this again and again during a sideways market.

# Chapter 3: Finding the Perfect Stock

When you are thinking of buying a stock, first spend some time watching it trade.

How does it respond to its own news flow, or to general market news?

Does it blast through round numbers (like 30, 40, etc.) and never look back, or does it have a difficult time punching through these ceilings?

You want to buy only the best stocks-- those that respond well to bad news, as well as good news.

Most traders don't know how to buy low and sell high. It is often easier to buy high, and sell higher. Don't be afraid to buy stocks that are hitting new all-time highs on good volume. Every long uptrend includes hundreds of points at which a stock is hitting new all-time highs.

The best trades are usually those in which everything lines up perfectly: the general market is in an uptrend, the stock is trading technically well (in a clear uptrend, constantly hitting new highs), and the stock's fundamentals are good (high revenue or earnings growth, positive earnings surprises, etc.).

Don't be afraid of high P/E stocks that are hitting new highs. Investors with a bias against high P/E stocks have missed out on many of the greatest winners of all time.

The best trades are usually the ones with a technically perfect set-up, where you also hate the stock or are afraid of it. If everyone hates a stock, it means that everyone has already sold the stock, and there is only one direction that the stock can go (which is UP).

Always remember that it is only price that pays. If a stock does not go where it should, it doesn't matter how right you are.

When a stock closes below its lower Bollinger Band, it should always get your attention.

If a stock is trading below its lower Bollinger Band, and the majority of traders are bearish on the stock, then you have the perfect set-up for a stock that has a high probability of snapping back to the middle band.
Look for stocks that are trending (in terms of user interest) on StockTwits.com. This is often a good way to find stocks that are oversold, or in nice uptrends or downtrends.

Buy stocks that hold up well during a market correction. If the market is down and your stock is flat or up slightly, it should continue to outperform when the market recovers.

This is because the stock is most likely being accumulated by institutions who have been supporting the stock, and buying on dips. Stocks with good relative strength like this will often go up much more when the market begins to recover.

Every bull market has its "market leaders." In the Dot-com bubble days, it was Yahoo, Sun Microsystems,

America Online, and Oracle, among others. In the most recent bull market it has been the so-called FANG stocks: Facebook, Apple, Netflix, and Google.

Market leaders always hold up well during market corrections, and then break out ahead of other stocks during market recoveries.

However, during a true bear market, the market leaders will often sell off 50-90% from their highs. This is why it is so important not to trade against the trend, especially during a bear market.

In a bear market, the previous market leaders will often lead on the way down, just as they had led on the way up.

Market leaders in a new bull market are rarely those from a previous bull market.

To find market leaders, look to see which industries are leading the stock market's advance. Is it tech, financials, energy, etc.? Then look for the strongest stocks within each strong industry. These are often the first stocks to break out after a market correction, or they are constantly hitting new 52-week or all-time highs.

You will rarely find stock momentum apart from industry momentum.

Small cap stocks (under $200 million market cap) and stocks with a small float will often have the most explosive moves. They can easily go up 20-50% in a week or two.

Screen for small cap stocks that are hitting new 52-week highs.

You can also screen for stocks that are up 100% in the last few months. These stocks will often continue their moves much further than anyone expects.

Remember that all that you need to get a big move in a stock is an imbalance of supply and demand. If there is huge demand for a stock, and limited supply, the stock will move up sharply.

There is a naturally limited supply of shares for a recent IPO with a small float. If institutional investors (mutual funds, hedge funds, etc.) get interested in the stock, the increased demand (coupled with the limited supply) can cause a huge run-up in prices.

If there is limited demand for a stock, and a huge supply of the shares, the stock will be forced lower. This can often happen after the six-month lock-up of an IPO, when insiders are finally able to sell their shares again.

Over the short term, supply and demand of shares will always trump fundamentals.

So will central bank actions. Whenever the Fed (or any central bank) does quantitative easing (or prints money), stock will go up globally. Analysts and economists don't like to hear this, but it's true.

# Chapter 4: Insider Secrets of the Stock Market

Reaction to the news is always more important than the news itself.

Let me repeat this point, because it is so essential to understand:

**Reaction to the news is always more important than the news itself.**

If a stock that has had a big run-up falls on a good earnings report, it is a sign that the uptrend may be over.

On the other hand, if a stock rallies when bad news is reported, the bad news is probably already priced into the stock, and the stock may continue to rise.

Markets have a tendency to over-discount identified risks, and under-discount unidentified risks. Whenever you keep hearing about a risk in the news, it is most likely completely priced into the stock or stock market. It is the risks that you are not hearing about, or that seem absurdly unlikely, that are the most dangerous.

If everyone is talking about something, it's already priced into the market. That means that the stock has already moved to where it needs to be. To make money in trading, you need to skate to where the puck is going to be, not where it has been.

Don't ignore the macro. If there is a housing bubble or a credit bubble, it will affect the pricing of everything. The market may ignore the risks for a long time, but when it finally focuses on the risk, watch out below.

The stock market is rarely rational. Sometimes it interprets everything positively, and sometimes everything negatively. Pay special attention to when that flips, and prepare for a change in the trend.

What causes a stock to trend over various time horizons?

Short-term price trends are driven by momentum and the short-term supply/demand of shares, as we have discussed.

Medium-term price trends are driven by earnings growth.

Long-term price trends are driven by business, social, and economic trends.

The stock market is in a strong uptrend (bull market) when the SPY, QQQ, and IWM are all trading above their 50-day moving averages, and their 50-day moving averages are trading above their 200-day moving averages. In this kind of environment, you can often take a more aggressive stance and make some serious money.

The stock market is in a strong downtrend (bear market) when the SPY, QQQ, and IWM are all trading below their 50-day moving averages, and their 50-day moving averages are trading below their 200-day moving averages. In this environment, you are often better off being in cash. If you try to go short, you may get blown away by a short-covering rally, which can be especially fierce and violent in a bear market. I discuss these issues in more depth in "Chapter 5: How to Trade a Bear Market."

Volume never lies. A stock that is hitting new 52-week or all-time highs on higher than average volume is a high probability bet. Especially if it has a market cap of $4 billion or less, or a small float (where the float is 20% or less of the total shares outstanding). And especially if the SPY, QQQ, and IWM are all in a bull market.

Stocks that have had their IPO ("initial public offering") in the last 6 months are especially nice trading vehicles, and often have small floats. Be careful, however: 6 months after the IPO, many insider lockups expire, and insiders may dump their shares onto the market, forcing down the price of the stock.

The stock market has a fractal character. A chart with 30-minute bars will look similar to a chart with daily bars, which will look similar to a chart of weekly bars. The same indicators may be used on any time interval chart.

You should try to pick the time frame that makes you most comfortable. If you like placing a trade and then going to the beach, trade daily or weekly bars. If you want more excitement and action, you can trade 15-minute or 30-minute bars.

Learn the most important candlestick chart formations, which will be helpful on any time frame chart. "Hammer" candlesticks often mark the end of a downtrend, just as "Shooting Stars" often mark the end of an uptrend. Bearish and bullish engulfing patterns are also useful for catching reversals. I have a whole section on the most important candlestick formations in my paid course at http://www.trader-university.com/

Here's an easy way to make money that usually works, even though it doesn't make any sense. If a stock is trading in the 90's for the first time, especially in the high 90's, it will almost always go to 100. Buy the stock in the 90's and immediately enter your sell limit order at 100.

Always look at the monthly chart of a stock or stock index to get the big picture. Pay special attention to regions of consolidation (sideways or range-bound trading), as well as breakouts and breakdowns. Is the monthly chart trending or sideways?

A daily close above the upper Bollinger Band (use a daily period=80) is always a sign that the stock should be closely examined. It means that something unusual has happened, in order for the stock to be trading two standard deviations away from its mean.

If trader sentiment on the stock is extremely bullish, and the indices are toppy, then the stock may a good short candidate.

If trader sentiment on the stock is not overly bullish, and if traders are denying that the stock can move higher, then you are more likely at the beginning of an uptrend. Go long and use the middle Bollinger Band as your trailing stop.

Remember not to avoid a stock just because it has a high P/E (price to earnings ratio). Many of the market's biggest winners began their run-ups with high P/E's and ended at even higher P/E's.

When the trend turns down, however, stay away. There are few things more dangerous than a high P/E stock whose earnings or revenue growth has slowed. Just because it has just gapped down 10% does not mean that it cannot trade much, much lower.

Short sellers are usually correct in the long run. You can play high short-interest stocks for short squeezes, but don't stick around too long, as these companies are usually fundamentally flawed.

A market that fails to move higher will usually go down. A stock will always search out our vulnerabilities, and move in such a way as to cause the maximum amount of pain to the maximum number of traders.

Never place a trade based on something you have just read in Barron's, Forbes, or The Wall Street Journal. Huge amounts of money have been lost by following their advice. Everyone is reading those sites every day, and so they are almost always just consensus wisdom.

Never buy a stock based on an analyst upgrade, or sell a stock based on an analyst downgrade. Analysts are lagging indicators. All of the good analysts have already quit and are running their own hedge funds. The bad ones are left behind.

Run, don't walk, when a company does a reverse split, or if the CFO resigns.

Never buy a penny stock that has been recommended by a co-worker or friend.

To increase your potential returns (and also your potential risk), try purchasing at-the-money call options on a stock that is in a smooth uptrend. These calls will often be underpriced (due to low implied volatility) if the stock has been trending up smoothly.

Or pick a reasonable price target for the trending stock, and purchase deep-out-of-the-money calls on the stock at a strike price that is 5 or 10 points below your price target. This kind of strategy has a low win/lose ratio, but a very high potential payout. I discuss a similar strategy in my book Learn to Trade Momentum Stocks at www.trader-books.com

A much more conservative options strategy is selling covered calls on a stock. This is an excellent way to profit from a stock that is trading sideways, especially if it is a good blue-chip consumer stock with a dividend yield that is greater than 3%. I discuss this strategy in great detail in my book Covered Calls Made Easy at www.trader-books.com

During a bull market, the VXX is an excellent short. Because of contango in the VIX futures, this volatility ETF loses a little bit of its value almost every day. It is constantly on its way down to zero—that is until a new bear market or market correction begins. Never be short the VXX when the 50-day moving average of the SPY crosses below its 200-day moving average.

Is there a quick trick to valuing a stock for a longer term investment? Simply estimate where earnings per share (EPS) will be in 5 years from now. Slap a 15 multiple (P/E) on that number and you have a reasonable price target for the stock. Warren Buffett uses a similar trick all the time.

Let's say that you are extremely lazy. If you do nothing else but buy the SPY (the ETF for the S&P 500) whenever it is down 40-50% from its highs and then sell it 4 or 5 years later, you will do very well indeed.

But if you choose to be an active trader, don't overcomplicate things. Trading is easy. Just buy the strongest stocks that keep moving up. Add to your winners, kick the losers out of your portfolio, and don't get too greedy. It's really that simple.

# Chapter 5: How to Trade a Bear Market

You will often hear that it is impossible to predict a bear market.

While this is true, it **is** possible to notice the beginnings of a bear market.

We cannot predict the future, but we can react to its gradual unfolding.

The truth is that bear markets do not come out of nowhere.

In fact, every bear market begins with many stocks' 50-day moving averages crossing below their 200-day moving averages. Major stock indices (SPY, QQQ, DIA, and IWM) will also see their 50-day moving averages cross below their 200-day moving averages.

While we cannot predict a bear market, we can certainly protect ourselves against one by exiting long positions when a stock's 50-day moving average crosses below its 200-day moving average.

If we are aggressive traders, we can even profit from such a downturn, by going short.

Stocks that have strong momentum on the way up often have even stronger momentum on the way down.

A stock that ran from 10 to 200 over three years might come crashing back down to 10 in a matter of 12 months. Many momentum stocks end up giving back all or most of their entire advance.

For example, in the bear market of 2000-2002, many momentum stocks declined 80-90% from their highs.

Near the end of a momentum stock's long uptrend, it will frequently be trading at a truly irrational P/E multiple. No amount of business success or growth will ever be able to justify such a multiple.

On the way up, no one cares, because everyone is making money.

But when a stock's upward momentum begins to slow, or even reverse, investors turn once again to the stock's valuation, realize how crazy it is, and decide to sell their shares. This selling helps to accelerate the stock's downward move.

Cisco Systems (CSCO) is a perfect example of this dynamic at work:

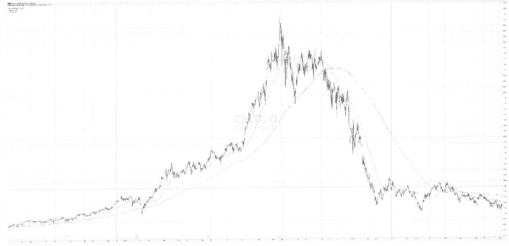

You can also access this image at the following link:
www.tradingview.com/x/jKTRuhwm/

For CSCO, the 50-day moving average crossed above the 200-day moving average on June 27, 1997 when the stock was trading at a split-adjusted price of just 7.39.

The stock proceeded to run for the next two and a half years, topping out at split-adjusted high of 82.00 and a P/E of almost 174!

The 50-day moving average finally crossed back below the 200-day moving average on October 4, 2000, at a split-adjusted closing price of 58.56.

When this happened, the stock promptly fell another 86%, finally bottoming out at split-adjusted low of 8.12 on October 8, 2002.

After a tremendous run of over 1000%, the stock retraced almost completely.

Almost everyone was surprised both by how far the stock rallied, and by how far it retraced—everyone, that is, except for the trend-followers who captured the majority of the move up and the move down.

So how does one short a momentum stock?

First, never be foolish enough to short a momentum stock until the 50-day moving average has closed below the 200-day moving average. Many otherwise very smart traders have lost their shirts trying to short stocks like Cisco on the way up. The stock was certainly overvalued, but it kept going up.

Second, look for stocks that have had tremendous run-ups, but whose revenue growth is beginning to slow.

The market is very quick to punish high-flying stocks whose growth begins to slow.

Shorting stocks can be quite risky, and is therefore not for everyone.

That being said, if you are able to bear the risks, the remainder of this chapter will teach you how.

To short a stock, it is first necessary for the stock to be available to "borrow" from your broker. If you cannot find a broker who will lend you the stock from its inventory, it is impossible to short the stock.

Once you have been able to borrow shares of the stock, you sell the shares into the market ("sell short" is the broker's order that you want to use). At the end of your trade, you will buy back the shares ("buy to cover") and deliver them back to your broker (this process of borrowing and delivery is usually automated, and is much easier than it sounds).

If the stock has declined, you will have made money. If the stock has gone up, you will have lost money.

In short selling, the key is to "sell high" and "buy low" (in that order!).

Short selling a momentum stock is further complicated by the fact that it can be tricky to figure out where to set your stop.

It is usually best to set a fairly wide stop of 10-20% (or even more) from entry. Thus, if you short a stock at 100 and are using a 20% stop, you will exit your short if the stock trades at 120.

The problem with shorting is that your maximum profit is 100%. For example, if you short a stock at 100 and it goes to zero, you have just made 100% (before commissions, which are minimal).

Unfortunately, you had to risk 10-20% (your stop loss) to put on this trade. At a 20% stop, **you are basically risking 1 dollar to make 5 dollars.**

On the long-side of momentum stocks, we are often risking 15% to make 300%. In other words, **we are risking 1 dollar to make 20 dollars.**

The risk-reward ratio of shorting is far inferior to that of going long.

For this reason, many traders will go on vacation at the beginning of a bear market. They will have made their money in the preceding bull market, and will see no reason to endure the stress of a bear market, where the risks far out-weigh the rewards.

To summarize, for those hardy souls who want to trade momentum stocks on the downside, there are 3 things to look for:

1) The 50-day moving average needs to close below the 200-day moving average for the stock.
2) The stock needs to have had a long run-up.
3) And preferably, the stock needs to show signs of slowing growth in revenue or earnings.

In the latter category, a stock will often have an earnings miss and gap down sharply when it reports slowing growth, or revenues or earnings that are below the market's expectations.

A textbook example of a successful short is the shoemaker Crocs (CROX) in late 2007. The stock had had a long run-up, from its IPO in February 2006, all the way to October 31, 2007.

On that day, after the market closed, Crocs reported disappointing earnings and projected 2008 revenue growth that fell short of the market's expectations.

How do we know that the earnings report fell short of Wall Street's high expectations, even if we don't know how to read an earnings transcript?

Simply based on the stock's reaction: it fell in the after-hours market and closed down 36% the following day.

You can also access the chart at the following link:
www.tradingview.com/x/NMm9yLS5/

Now most people would find it quite difficult to short a stock that had already fallen 36%. But we know that the time to short a momentum stock is when its momentum has sharply reversed, and not a moment before.

Then on January 2, 2008, the 50-day moving average closed below the 200-day moving average and the stock closed at 37.90. If you had gone short the following day at the market open at 38.00 and set your stop at 10%, you would have been able to ride the stock all the way down from 38.00 to 3.02 (which is where the stock was trading when the 50-day moving average finally crossed back above the 200-day moving average).

You made 92% on this trade, and risked only 10%. That is about as good as shorting can get.

There is one more thing that you should know about shorting momentum stocks. When you borrow shares of a stock from your broker that you wish to short, you will need to pay a fee that is based on how long you borrow the shares for. When many people are trying to short a certain stock, that stock will be on the "hard-to-borrow list"— meaning that it can be expensive to borrow the shares from a broker.

Sometimes these fees can be as high as 100% annualized. This means that if the stock that you have shorted goes to zero in one year, you make 100%, but need to pay your broker 100% (because the stock was hard-to-borrow and you held it for 1 year at an annualized 100% borrow rate).

High borrowing costs make it extremely important to time your entry correctly (using the 50/200 moving average crossover method that we have discussed). As we have seen, the stock needs to fall faster than your borrow rate, or you will end up losing money even if the trade itself makes money.

For example, if you have borrowed the stock at a 100% annualized borrow rate, and it falls 50% in 3 months, you are still OK. You make 50% on the stock short, and only have to pay 25% in borrowing costs (100%/12 months times 3 months= 25%), for a net return of 50% - 25% = 25%.

Even worse, when you are short a stock, it is possible for the broker to ask for the shares back at any time. If this occurs (and it almost always occurs at the worst possible time), you will need to cover your short (buy back the shares in the open market) wherever it happens to be trading on that day.

When shorts are forced to cover by their brokers, a stock will typically rally significantly, so that you will probably be buying back your shares at a loss.

When you are just starting out, trade all of your stocks from the long side only.

Exit your long positions when the 50-day moving average crosses below the 200-day moving average, and don't try to get short. You will make plenty of money on the long side, and avoid all of the complications and stresses associated with shorting stocks.

When a bear market begins, take all of your chips off the table and go hang out on a tropical beach somewhere. You'll be glad that you did.

While on the beach, you may allow yourself to check the market just once a week.

A bear market is often a good time to switch from being a trader to being a value investor.

Value investing is simply the strategy of purchasing a stock when it is undervalued. A value investor will compare a company's normalized earnings to its current market value, to determine if a stock is undervalued.

Value investing can be difficult during a bull market. For newbie traders, it is often easier to trade momentum than value.

But during a bear market, it is often wise to stop trading and to begin to look for good entries in undervalued stocks.

Warren Buffett is a master of this technique.

For example, in the middle of the 2008 financial crisis, Buffett wrote:

"A simple rule dictates my buying: be fearful when others are greedy, and be greedy when others are fearful."

and

"Bad news is an investor's best friend. It lets you buy a slice of America's future at a marked-down price."

The easiest time to buy a great business at a great price is during a bear market.

In 2008, Coke had earnings per share (EPS) of $1.51. In 2009, Coke traded as low as 18.70, on a split-adjusted basis. At that price, Coke had a trailing P/E (price to earnings ratio) of just 12.38, an earnings yield (earnings divided by market capitalization) of 8.08%, and a dividend yield of 4.39%.

By comparison, today Coke has a P/E of 25.00, an earnings yield of 4.00%, and a dividend yield of 3.40%. The stock has more than doubled from its lows, all while paying a healthy dividend every year.

Anyone could have bought Coke below $20 in 2009, but very few did. It did not require inside information, or stock tips. All that it required was nerves of steel to buy when it appeared that the financial world was ending.

How long into a bear market should one wait to buy a great business?

One method is just to wait for the dividend yield to get to 4%, or the trailing P/E (calculated using the company's last 12 months of earnings) to get to 15 or lower on a stock like Coke. That is the "valuation method."

The second method is the "market timing" method. It involves waiting a fixed period of time into a bear market before buying-- or waiting for a large peak to trough draw down in price.

For example, Coke peaked at 44.47 (split-adjusted) in July 1998. It fell until March 2003, trading as low as 18.50. In other words, it fell roughly 58% from peak to trough.

Again, Coke peaked at 32.79 in January 2008, before the financial crisis really got started. It fell until March 2009, trading as low as 18.72. In other words, it fell roughly 43% from peak to trough.

Using this "market timing" method, you would wait for Coke to sell off 40-50% from its last highest price, and then buy your position.

Since Coke is a blue-chip stock that is included in indices like the Dow Jones Industrial Average and the S&P 500, it tends to bottom at the same time that the general stock market bottoms.

The 2000-2002 bear market lasted roughly 2 years and 7 months.  The 2008-2009 bear market lasted roughly 1 year and 4 months.

Let's say that the stock market peaks and then falls for more than 1 year.  Further, there is plenty of pessimism on TV, in the newspapers and on the internet, and all of your friends are selling their stocks.

**That** is the time that you want to be loading up on businesses like Coke, especially if they have fallen over 40% from their peaks, have P/E's of 15 or less, and have dividend yields approaching or exceeding 4%.

A time like this will come again.  I do not know if it will happen in 2017 or 2018, but it is certain to come.  The current bull market has been running since March 2009.  We are well overdue for a bear market.

# Chapter 6: The Winning Trader's Mindset

Trading success always begins with acquiring the right mindset.

To become a successful trader, the first thing you need to know is yourself. Learn to step outside of yourself and watch your own reactions like an outside observer.

90% of trading is learning to master your own psychology. You can lie to your boss, you can lie to your wife, but you can never lie to the market. It will always call you out.

Trading is the closest that you will ever get to the pure and unvarnished truth. Everyone else lies to you. Only the market tells the truth.

If you lose money, you are wrong. If you make money, you are right. It's that simple.

If you like to lie to yourself, trading is not for you. The market will tell you the truth in a way that is very unpleasant to hear.

The trader Ed Seykota is famous for saying:

"Win or lose, everybody gets what they want out of the market. Some people seem to like to lose, so they win by losing money."

To become a successful trader, you have to be willing to make mistakes on a regular basis, without beating yourself up or becoming discouraged.  If you make a mistake, take a quick small loss, and move on to the next trade.

Don't time travel: don't dwell on past bad trades, or fantasize about future great trades.  Allow trading to teach you to live in the present.

How you start each morning also determines your trading mindset.  Begin the day with prayer or meditation, and some simple stretches, or a short walk outside.

Emotional resilience is essential to becoming a great trader.  The only way to remain emotionally resilient is to sleep at least 8 hours every night, exercise every day, and eat healthy foods.  An unhealthy trader is a bad trader.

When a trader with money meets a trader with experience, the trader with experience gets the money, and the trader with money gets the experience.

Always trade like a sniper, not a machine gunner.  Wait patiently for your target to come into view, and only then pull the trigger.  Don't take just any trade out of boredom.  This is a game in which patience is rewarded.

Your goal is to squeeze the profit out of a stock, and then to move on.  There are always stocks that are making big moves, so why hold on to a stock that is not making you money?

You don't need to make back the money that you lost on the same stock.  If you would not buy the stock right here, you probably should not still own it.

Make sure that you know why you are trading. If you are just trading for the thrill and excitement, you will lose money. If you are just trading for the money, you will lose money. But if you are trading to honestly improve your character, you will make money.

When we are learning to trade, we have a choice when we encounter an obstacle. Will we allow it to block our way?

Or will we use it as a learning experience, and have the strength to move on? For great traders, the obstacle is the way.

Our perceptions often determine our abilities. If you think that you cannot do something, you have ensured that it will be impossible.

Do not allow yourself to entertain bad thoughts. Entertain only positive thoughts, and your actual abilities will be mysteriously enhanced.

Whenever you have a choice in the markets, always do the hardest thing. The easiest thing to do is rarely the most profitable.

Don't take losses personally. They are not a reflection on your character. Learn to treat your trading like a business: losses are just part of the game.

Never try to play catch up during a losing streak. It is better to take a week or two off, than to try to make back the money right away. If you are trading badly, stop trading immediately.

To succeed in trading, you must completely forget about the money.

Focus instead on getting your entry point right, focus on your stop loss, and focus on your profit target. Do these things, and the money will take care of itself.

If you want to make a quantum leap in your trading, start by never placing a trade without a solid, quantifiable reason for doing so.

You can never force the market to give you anything. Rather you must learn to listen carefully to find out what the market has to offer you.

Don't trade when your head is not in the game. You will only lose money.

Keep your ego out of the game. When you place a trade solely to impress other people, you will lose money.

Don't talk to your screen and tell the market what to do. It can't hear you. And it doesn't care.

Don't blame anyone or anything for your trading losses. When you've learned to take responsibility for your losers, you will be ready to have big winning trades.

A lazy trader always loses lots of money in the long run. You need to treat your trading like a job, and take it seriously.

To be successful, you need to learn how to run your trading like a business.

# Chapter 7: How to Run Your Trading like a Business

Start with a good computer, a fast internet connection, and a comfortable desk and chair.  You don't need one of those expensive, multi-monitor computer set-ups like every day trader had in the 1990's.  But don't skimp on computer RAM and a high-speed internet connection.

Next, if you really want to run your trading like a business, you must realize that you can no longer trade by the seat of your pants.  You will need to invest in your trader education.

To make money in the markets, you first need a "trading edge."

A trading edge is simply an approach to the stock market that gives you an advantage over the other players in the stock market.  If you don't know what your trading edge is, you probably don't have one.

I have provided many elements of a trading edge in chapters 2-5 of this book, and in my other books.

To further develop your trading edge, you should read as many books about the stock market as you can.  Start with my books at www.trader-books.com

Then watch all of my free videos on my YouTube Channel "Trader University."

If you want to shorten your learning curve and learn how to start making money right away, you can also take my

paid course "Learn to Trade Stocks like a Pro" at
http://www.trader-university.com/

But don't stop there. Keep reading trading books by other
authors. Explore other trading videos on YouTube. Hang
out on StockTwits.com to get more ideas. Read as many
blogs about trading and investing as you can.

The more you learn, the more that you will be able to
learn. It is a virtuous circle.

After you find your trading edge, you will then need to
develop a "trading plan."

A trading plan is simply a plan that tells you these four
things **in advance**:

1. When to enter a trade (entry signal)
2. When to exit a trade with a profit (exit signal, or
   profit target)
3. When to exit a trade with a loss (stop loss)
4. How big to size a position

Losing traders do not have a trading plan, and trade solely
based on their emotions.

Winning traders always have a trading plan, and stick to it,
regardless of their emotions.

Panic is the enemy of all traders; only by having a clear
mind and a trading plan can we prevail when others are
panicking.

Never exit a trade because of your fears.  There are only 4 good reasons to exit a trade:

1.  Your initial stop loss is hit.
2.  Your trailing stop loss is hit.
3.  Your profit target is hit.
4.  Your time stop loss is hit.

Let's examine each of these in turn.

## Initial Stop Losses

You should always know where you are getting out before you enter into a trade.

Pick a place on the chart where the stock should clearly never go, if you are correct about the trade.  That is where you should place your stop.  Then size your position such that you will not lose more than 1-2% of your account if that stop is hit.

When you enter a trade, write down your stop loss and profit target on a piece of paper, and keep it next to your computer.  Look at the paper whenever you are about to do something rash.

Use a wider initial stop loss for volatile stocks, and a tighter initial stop loss for less volatile stocks.  In other words, your stop should be closer for a stock like Coke, and further away for a stock like Tesla.

Never enter your stop orders directly into the market.  The market has a way of sniffing out stops and running them.

Pick a stop loss level, write it down on a piece of paper by your computer, and then get out immediately (using a limit order) if the stock trades at your stop loss level.

In trading, honoring a stop loss is like knowing when to fold in poker. A small loss lets you live to fight another day.

Never let a losing trade get out of hand. Nip it in the bud while it is still a small loss. A large loss may put you out of the game for good.

## Trailing Stops

After you buy a stock, if the stock moves up and your trade becomes profitable, then move your stop loss to your entry price. If the stock continue to move higher, slowly move your stop higher. If you follow these rules, you will always cut your losers short, and let your winners run.

Parabolic SAR, 5-bar or 10-bar exponential moving averages, and 20-bar moving averages all make excellent trailing stops. Pick one and learn to use it before you move on to the next one.

## Profit Targets

If you are riding the trend, you should usually wait until the trend reverses to exit a stock. This will maximize your big winners, which is where most of your profits will be made.

However, if a stock starts to go parabolic (i.e. straight up), you should get ready to take profits. You can always sell 1/10 of your position over the next 10 trading days, and thus scale out.

If you are trading mean reversion (e.g. a rubber band stock snapping back), you should set your profit target at the middle Bollinger Band.

## Time Stop Losses

A time stop loss is the decision (made before placing a trade) when to exit the trade if the stock does nothing. Money in a stock that is not moving is dead money. If a stock is still not moving 3-5 days after your entry, you are better off exiting and looking for a stock that is moving.

Always honor your stop losses. If you don't learn to take small losses, you will eventually take a massive loss.

Never risk more than 1% to 2% of your capital on a single trade.

If you lose 20% of your account on a trade, you will need to make 25% to get back to even. If you lose 50% of your account on a trade, you will need to make 100% to get back to even. This is why it is so important not to let losses get out of hand.

As Warren Buffett is fond of saying, there are two main rules:

Rule #1: Never lose money.
Rule #2: Never forget Rule #1.

90% of your losses will come from 10% of your trades.

90% of your profits will also come from 10% of your trades.

Remember that great traders are reactive, not predictive. They do not try to predict where a stock is going, but they always know their potential entry price, target price, and stop loss price. Great traders let the market tell them what to do.

Great trading is not about predicting tomorrow's weather, but rather about being able to notice that it is raining today.

Good trading is about probabilities, not prognostication. If you have a small edge, and keep placing bets, you will win in the long run.

Don't focus on the money; focus on trading your plan.

Trading is all about good risk management, controlling your ego, focus, and dedication. If you don't love this game, you'll probably lose money to someone who does.

Knowing when to sit on your hands is half the battle in trading. Good trading should consist of more watching than trading.

If there are no attractive trading set-ups, do nothing. Go for a jog instead.

But when there is an opportunity to be had, make sure that you channel all of your time and energy towards your trading.

If the general markets (as measured by the SPY and QQQ) and an individual stock are both in uptrends, it is a good time to increase your position size and trade more aggressively.

The most money is made near the end of a trend when a stock goes parabolic and the public and pundits are in a state of disbelief. Enjoy the ride up, but don't expect it to last forever. Honor your trailing stop, or slowly sell out your position into the move up. Exit your entire position when trader sentiment gets too giddy and the major news outlets start to cover the stock too extensively.

Never hold a position that gaps sharply against you immediately after you have entered the trade. That type of situation never ends well.

If a stock sells off on good earnings, get out immediately.

You do not need to make your money back in the same stock where you lost it.

If you are holding on to a losing position, ask yourself this: "Would I buy the stock at today's price?" If the answer is no, you should sell the stock.

If you have a trade on that keeps you awake at night, it is either the wrong trade, or your position size is too large. Either scale back the position size, or get out entirely. Life is too short to lose sleep over a trade.

You can always get back into the stock after the stress has dissipated and you have a fresh perspective on it.

Remember that the market will always move in such a way as to cause the maximum pain to the maximum number of traders.

If a stock suddenly becomes much more volatile than usual, just get out, or at least sharply scale back your position in the stock.

If you ever have to go online to ask other traders whether you should hold on to a stock, you already know the answer. You need to get out completely and immediately, because you are so lost that you are asking complete strangers what to do.

Keep a trading journal. When you enter a trade, write down your rationale for the trade and your stop loss.

Review past trades to learn from your mistakes.

Did you follow your stop loss? Did you switch to a different rationale for the trade once it started losing money?

Did you hold on to a losing trade and turn it into a long-term investment, because you were afraid to take a loss?

When you are losing money, reduce your position size. If you keep losing, continue reducing your position size until you are on the sidelines.

When you are making money, you are allowed to increase your position size. But don't bet the farm. That usually results in losing the farm.

In trading, it is more important to play great defense than great offense. If you lose your capital, you are out of the game.

If you keep working at it and keep your losses under control, you will eventually become a great trader.

# Chapter 8: From Small Beginnings to Great Wealth

We've covered a lot of ground in this book. I hope that you are ready to take this information and use it to start making money for yourself trading.

The best way to learn about trading is just to start doing it. Start with very small positions, and then slowly increase them as your capital (and your confidence!) increases.

There's no better way to learn than simply by doing.

The biggest hurdle to becoming a successful trader is the failure to start.

The second biggest hurdle is the failure to continue. Most of us are tortoises, but the good news is that trading is a race that any tortoise can win.

Learning to trade is a marathon, not a sprint. Be patient with yourself, and give yourself the time to master one set-up or strategy before you move on to the next one. Slow and steady wins this race.

Also remember that your life is not a script that you are forced to follow. Once you realize that you are the author of the script, you will write yourself a heroic part to play.

The future is not something that just happens. The future is something that you make happen.

There's a reason that 90% of traders lose money. It's because they started trading with little or no preparation.

You can't become a lawyer or doctor without education. And the same goes for trading.

The best investment that you can make is an investment in your own trader education.

If you want to become an earning machine, you must first become a learning machine.

Lastly, remember that there is more to life than trading. Real happiness comes from our relationships, not from our money or possessions.

It's nice to become rich, but trading is ultimately not about the money. It is about the journey of self-discovery.

Making money is just a side-effect of discovering who you are. If you are not interested in self-discovery, the markets are an expensive place to hang out.

Let me assure you: if you can stick with the game, you will make money in the stock market.

And when you do, be sure to share your trading profits with those who are in need.

Often, the more money you share, the more money you will make. And the more money you make, the more you will be able to share. It is a virtuous circle.

I'm here to help you on your journey to becoming a professional trader.

If you have questions, or just want to say hi, write to me at matt@trader.university

I love to hear from my readers, and I answer every email personally.

Before you go, I'd like to say "thank you" for purchasing this book and reading it all the way to the end.

If you enjoyed this book and found it useful, I'd be very grateful if you'd post an honest review on Amazon. All you need to do is to go to www.trader-books.com and click on the correct book cover.

Then click the blue link next to the yellow stars that says "customer reviews." You'll then see a gray button that says "Write a customer review"—click that and you will be able to submit your review to Amazon.

**If you would like to learn more ways to make money in the markets, check out my other Kindle books on the next page.**

# Keep Learning With These Trading Books

**Rocket Stocks: Learn to Profit from the Stock Market's Biggest Winners**

**Invest Like Warren Buffett: Powerful Strategies for Building Wealth**

**Monthly Cash Machine:Powerful Strategies for Selling Options in Bull and Bear Markets**

**Covered Calls Made Easy**
**The Amazon #1 Bestseller for Options Trading**

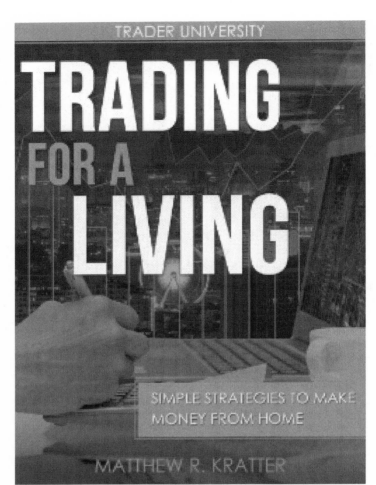

**Trading For A Living**

TRADER UNIVERSITY

# LEARN TO TRADE
# MOMENTUM
# STOCKS

**MAKE MONEY WITH
TREND FOLLOWING**

MATTHEW R. KRATTER

**Learn to Trade Momentum Stocks**

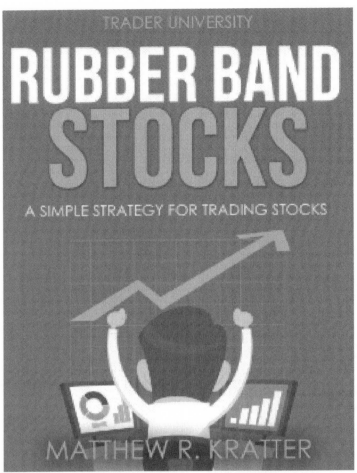

**Rubber Band Stocks: A Simple Strategy for Trading Stocks**

# Your Free Gift

Thanks for purchasing my book!

As a way of showing my appreciation, I've created a **FREE BONUS CHAPTER** that includes even more trading strategies and market wisdom.

In this Bonus Chapter, you will learn:

- The single most important factor that drives the markets in the short term
- How to profit from the stock market's seasonality
- What happens to the stock market when all experts agree
- How to pick the best stock in a given industry
- And much, much more

Enter your email at the link below, and I will send you a free copy of this Bonus Chapter:

## http://www.trader.university/secrets

# About the Author

Hi there!

My name is Matthew Kratter. I am the founder of www.trader.university, and the best-selling author of multiple books on trading and investing. I have more than 20 years of trading experience, including working at multiple hedge funds.

Most individual traders and investors are at a huge disadvantage when it comes to the markets. Most are unable to invest in hedge funds. Yet, when they trade their own money, they are competing against computer algorithms, math PhD's, and multi-billion dollar hedge funds. I've been on the inside of many hedge funds. I know how professional traders and investors think and approach the markets. And I am committed to sharing their trading strategies with you in my books and courses.

When I am not trading or writing new books, I enjoy bodysurfing and otherwise hanging out at the beach with my wife, kids, and labradoodle.

If you enjoyed this book, you might also enjoy my other books, which are available here:

http://www.trader-books.com

Or send me an email at matt@trader.university. I would love to hear from you.

# Disclaimer

While the author has used his best efforts in preparing this book, he makes no representations or warranties with respect to the accuracy or completeness of the contents of this book and specifically disclaims any implied warranties or merchantability or fitness for a particular purpose. The advice and strategies contained herein may not be suitable for your situation. You should consult with a legal, financial, tax, or other professional where appropriate. Neither the publisher nor the author shall be liable for any loss of profit or any other commercial damages, including but not limited to special, incidental, consequential, or other damages.

This book is for educational purposes only. The views expressed are those of the author alone, and should not be taken as expert instruction or commands. The reader is responsible for his or her own actions.

Adherence to all applicable laws and regulations, including international, federal, state, and local laws, is the sole responsibility of the purchaser or reader.

Neither the author nor the publisher assumes any responsibility or liability whatsoever on the behalf of the purchaser or reader of these materials.

Any perceived slight of any individual or organization is purely unintentional.

Past performance is not necessarily indicative of future performance. Forex, futures, stock, and options trading is

Made in United States
Orlando, FL
20 December 2021

12194093R10043